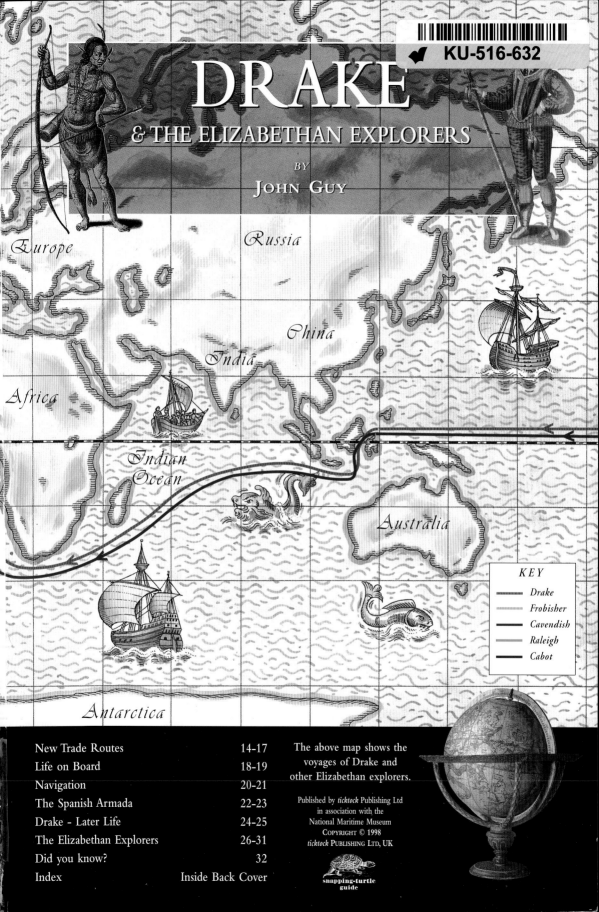

DRAKE
& THE ELIZABETHAN EXPLORERS

BY
JOHN GUY

Europe

Russia

China

India

Africa

Indian
Ocean

Australia

Antarctica

KEY

Drake
Frobisher
Cavendish
Raleigh
Cabot

The above map shows the
voyages of Drake and
other Elizabethan explorers.

Published by *ticktock* Publishing Ltd
in association with the
National Maritime Museum
COPYRIGHT © 1998
ticktock PUBLISHING LTD, UK

snapping-turtle
guide

Drake ~ the Early Years

The name of Sir Francis Drake is best identified with England's defeat of the Spanish Armada, his circumnavigation of the world and with stories of heroic raids upon the Spaniards in the Caribbean. As with so many heroes, however, the story is more complex. Francis Drake was born to a humble farming family in Devon and might have become a farmer himself had his father not been an outspoken Protestant lay preacher who was forced to leave his home, with his family, and seek safe refuge in Kent. They lived for some years on board a hulk moored on the River Medway, which no doubt fired the imagination of the young Francis. He was apprenticed to the owner and captain of a small coaster that traded between England and Holland. His distant cousin John Hawkins secured him a position as purser on a slave-trading voyage and he soon rose to the rank of captain.

DEFENDING THE FLEET

When Drake's father arrived in Kent he became a lay preacher to the seamen in Chatham Dockyard, living with his family on a hulk moored on the River Medway. In 1560 he became vicar of Upchurch, a nearby small riverside village. The young Francis first learned his seafaring skills on the Medway. The picture above shows Upnor Castle, built by Elizabeth I in 1559-67 to defend the new dockyard at Chatham.

CHILDHOOD HOME

Francis Drake was born in a small farm cottage at Crowndale, near Tavistock in Devon, some time between 1539 and 1545, the eldest of 12 children. His father, Edmund, had been a sailor but had settled on his brother John's farm in 1544. This statue was later erected in Tavistock in honour of Drake's achievements.

DRAKE'S ISLAND

Following riots by Catholics in the West Country in 1549, Edmund Drake was forced to leave his home with his family and seek refuge on St.Nicholas's Island, in Plymouth Harbour. From there, his relative William Hawkins arranged for his safe removal to Kent. The island was afterwards known as 'Drake's Island' to commemorate the event.

LANDED GENTRY

Following his knighthood in 1581, Drake boosted his status by claiming to be descended from a Devonshire landed family of that name. He had their coat of arms displayed aboard his ship, the *Golden Hind*

SIR FRANCIS DRAKE
– A Time Line –

~1492~
Columbus's first voyage to the West Indies.

~1519~
Magellan sets out on first circumnavigation of the world.

~1533~
Princess Elizabeth (later Elizabeth I) is born.

~1534~
Cartier's first voyage to Newfoundland.

~c.1535~
Martin Frobisher born.

A TRADE OF MISERY

John Hawkins, a prominent figure in Elizabeth's navy, began his illustrious career (like Drake himself and many others) engaged in the slave trade in 1562. Drake's first such voyage was as purser aboard one of Hawkins's ships in 1566. The voyage itself ended in disaster, but Drake went on to become an officer serving with Hawkins on a later slave-trading trip and in 1568 took command of his first ship.

IRISH REVOLTS

In 1573, on his return from a particularly successful raid on Spanish ships in the Caribbean, Drake was obliged to go to Ireland rather than return home. Elizabeth had struck a temporary peace with Spain and his presence in England would have been an embarrassment. He stayed there for three years, helping Walter Devereux, 1st Earl of Essex, put down Irish opposition to English colonisation. The mission failed, eventually leading to open revolt, when many English settlers were killed.

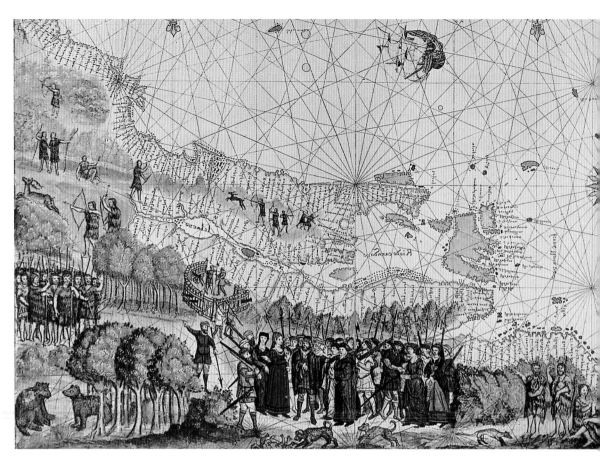

JACQUES CARTIER (1491-1557)

Jacques Cartier was a French explorer, commissioned by the king of France to search for possible sites for new settlements in North America and for a North-West Passage. He made several memorable excursions into the waterways around north-east America and in 1534 circumnavigated the Gulf of St. Lawrence. This was then thought to be a gateway to the Pacific but turned out to be a huge bay off eastern Canada. He is seen here on a later expedition in 1542, landing on the banks of the mighty St. Lawrence river. Cartier's explorations led to the later French claims on Canada.

SIR FRANCIS DRAKE
-A TIME LINE-

~1541~
Probable year of Drake's birth at Tavistock, Devon.

~1545~
Henry VIII's ship the
Mary Rose *sinks.*

~1547~
Henry VIII dies and is succeeded by Edward VI.

~1549~
Cranmer's English Prayer Book published; leads to Catholic riots.

Drake family (Protestants) forced to leave Devon for Kent.

INHOSPITABLE SEAS

The seas of the northern Atlantic and Arctic Oceans are very inhospitable. Icebergs were a particular problem and vast areas iced over completely in winter. This made it difficult for early explorers to chart the northern coasts of America and Russia. Ironically, what none of them knew was that the search for both the North-East and North-West Passages ultimately led to the same place (later named the Bering Strait) which is the only passage into the northern Pacific, between Alaska and Siberia.

The Search for the N.E.&N.W. Passages

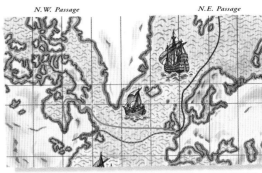

N.W. Passage   *N.E. Passage*

Frobisher (1576) ▬ *Barents (1596)* ▬ *Hudson (1610-11)* ▬ *Cartier (1534-6)*

*T*ogether Spain and Portugal controlled the southern seaways, forcing other nations to search for an alternative route to reach the Pacific Ocean and the fabled riches of China and south-east Asia. Two possibilities emerged: the North-East Passage, traversing the northern coasts of Russia, and the North-West Passage, passing around the northern coasts of North America. Drake himself tried unsuccessfully to locate the North-West Passage, from the Pacific side, in 1578. Having completed his mission to attack Spanish ports on the west coast of South America, he struck north to find a way home, but was forced back across the Pacific and so sailed home round the world, though that was never his original intention. Several navigators in succeeding centuries managed to locate the strait between Alaska and Russia, but none was able to pass through it from the north west. The Norwegian explorer, Roald Amundsen, is generally accepted to be the first person to sail round northern Canada and through the Bering Strait in 1906, after a three-year expedition.

THE FUR TRADE

Denied the lucrative markets of China and the Far-East, merchants soon realised the potential of the fur trade (and later gold) to be found in North America. Large companies were established, such as the Hudson Bay Company, which made vast profits by buying animal pelts from the native Americans at very low prices and then exporting them to Europe.

HENRY HUDSON

Henry Hudson (d.1611) was an English navigator and explorer who was employed by the Dutch East India Company to search for the North-West Passage. After several attempts he reached the North American coast and discovered what are now known as the Hudson River, Strait and Bay. In 1611, after a winter spent ice-bound, his crew mutinied and cast him adrift in a small boat, along with eight others, and he was never seen again.

NEAR MISS

One of the problems facing 16th-century explorers was that the lands for which they were searching were complete unknown quantities, both in terms of location and size. When we trace the routes they followed we can see just how close to their objectives they sometimes got, without ever realising it. On his return journey home round the world, for example, Drake sailed a zig-zag course through the East Indies in a vain search for the Southern Continent, taking him tantalisingly close to Australia's northern coast.

SIR FRANCIS DRAKE
-A Time Line-

~1553~
Edward VI dies and is succeeded by Mary I.

Sir Hugh Willoughby leads expedition to find North-East Passage.

~1554~
Richard Chancellor reaches Moscow and establishes trade relations with Russia.

Mary I marries Philip of Spain.

~1558~
Mary I dies and is succeeded by Elizabeth I.

~1559~
Elizabeth I is crowned queen of England.

Elizabethan Prayer Book published.

~1560~
Catholicism outlawed in Scotland.

~1560~
Edmund Drake (Francis's father) takes up vicarage of Upchurch, Kent.

TRAVELLING IN STYLE

Drake's ship on his circumnavigation was originally called the *Pelican*, but he renamed it *Golden Hind* off South America, before attempting his epic voyage across the southern oceans. This was in honour of his patron sir Christopher Hatton, whose coat of arms included a hind. Drake enjoyed good living and often carried musicians to entertain him on the long months spent aboard ship.

CENTRE OF THE UNIVERSE

In Elizabethan times the other planets in our solar system were thought to revolve around the Earth. Armillary spheres were used to demonstrate the movements of the heavenly bodies and to show the relative positions of the equator, the tropics and the arctic and antarctic circles. After Magellan's expedition successfully circumnavigated the world, it became possible to calculate the Earth's size more accurately and to draw more precise navigational charts.

THE FIRST ENGLISHMAN IN JAPAN

The Elizabethan pilot and adventurer, Will Adams, set sail in 1598 with a Dutch expedition to south-east Asia. Only one of the five ships that setout survived, blown off course and eventually landing in Japan in 1600. Adams was taken prisoner but was later released on condition he taught the Japanese his seafaring skills. James Clavell's novel, *Shogun*, is based on Adams's exploits.

Quest for the Southern Continent

While few Europeans suspected the existence of North and South America in the 16th century (China was believed to lie due west across the Atlantic Ocean), legends abounded of a vast 'Southern Continent' somewhere in the South Atlantic, which many presumed to be the fabled lost continent of Atlantis. Several attempts at discovery were made, including by Drake on the return voyage of his circumnavigation. Explorers hoped to discover an inhabited and highly civilised land, where they could trade, but it remained elusive. At the same time, the merchant adventurers were also looking to forge trading links with south-east Asia, in particular the Spice Islands, China and Japan. The first Englishman to set foot in Japan was Will Adams. Born at Gillingham, in Kent, he learned his seafaring skills on the River Medway, like Drake before him. By the end of the 16th century Spain's 'golden age' was coming to a close. Most of the discoveries made after then were by English, Dutch and French expeditions.

ELUSIVE CONTINENT

Although a few explorers had made brief contact with the islands to the north of Australia, the existence of an inhabited southern continent eluded the Elizabethans. Tasman landed in Australia in 1642 (right) but it was not until the voyages of Captain Cook, 1768-80, that the existence of a vast, habitable continent (where we now know Antarctica to be), was finally disproved and the full outline of Australia confirmed.

Drake's Circumnavigation of the World...

*f*rancis Drake was only the second commander (and the first Englishman) successfully to circumnavigate the world. The main reason for Drake's epic journey, however, was not in the interests of scientific discovery but of trade and plunder, motivated by greed. At the time, Spain was the most powerful nation in Europe and jealously guarded the seaways to her lucrative new colonies. Elizabeth I commissioned Drake to sail across the southern Atlantic, through the Straits of Magellan, and attack Spanish treasure ships and settlements on South America's unprotected west coast. He then went on to cross the Pacific Ocean and reach the Spice Islands of the East Indies. Drake returned home a rich man, his successful circumnavigation being little more than a boost to his reputation.

'THE DRAGON'

Drake was a powerful personality and commanded respect wherever he went. Native peoples often paid homage to him and even the Spanish grudgingly referred to him as El Draque, 'the Dragon', supposedly blessed with magical powers.

LOST CIVILISATION

The Mayan civilisation of Central America flourished many centuries before Drake's circumnavigation. They evolved a sophisticated knowledge of astronomy and mathematics, but there is no evidence that Drake brought back any scientific discoveries from the cities he visited; like the Spanish he merely plundered their riches. The round tower shown here is an observatory at the Mexican city of Chichen Itza.

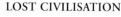

SPANISH GOLD

The Spaniards ruthlessly exploited the nations of Central and South America, plundering their riches. They melted down gold ornaments and set natives to work in gold and silver mines. The wealth they shipped back to Spain aroused the interest of Drake and the other Elizabethan privateers. The coins shown here are doubloons (meaning a double or two-escudo piece) the highest value Spanish coin at that time.

NEW ALBION

Drake called in at what is now San Francisco to refit his ships before commencing the return journey home. He had an audience with the local Indians, who invited him to become their king. He refused but did claim the area for England (calling it New Albion) though no English settlement was ever established there. The Spanish, who made several explorations up the Californian coast, did establish a small missionary settlement there by the bay, which they called San Francisco.

REPRISALS

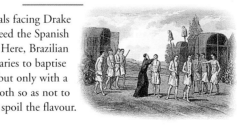

The dangers of native reprisals facing Drake and other explorers (and indeed the Spanish settlers) were ever-present. Here, Brazilian cannibals allow missionaries to baptise their prisoners but only with a damp cloth so as not to spoil the flavour.

AZTEC SPLENDOUR

This picture of Tenochtitlan, in Mexico, shows a pre-conquest view of the magnificent Aztec capital city. Although Drake never reached this far inland (concentrating his efforts on coastal ports) he was equally guilty as the Spaniards in plundering the riches of such ancient sites, principally gold.

SIR FRANCIS DRAKE
-A Time Line-

~1562~
John Hawkins's first successful slave-trade voyage to West Indies.

~1564~
William Shakespeare born.

~1565~
Tobacco first introduced into England - probably by John Hawkins.

~1566~
Drake's first voyage to the Caribbean as junior officer on Hawkins's third slave-trade voyage to Spanish Main.

~1568~
Mary Queen of Scots flees to England in exile.

The Hawkins/Drake slaving voyage ends in disaster at San Juan de Ulloa.

~1569~
Drake marries Mary Newman at St. Budeaux, near Plymouth.

~1570~
Drake sails for the coast of Panama and begins his reign of terror amongst Spanish shipping.

~1571~
Elizabeth I opens Royal Exchange in London.

~1572~
Drake sets out to take the Spanish port of Nombre de Dios, in Panama.

~1573~
Peace is agreed between England and Spain - Drake has to lie low with his spoils of war.

~1575~

Drake appears in Ireland as part of the Earl of Essex's campaign.

~1576~

Martin Frobisher attempts to find North-West Passage.

Drake returns from Ireland and plans his attack on the west coast of South America (which became his circumnavigation voyage).

~1577~

Drake sets out on his voyage round the world.

John Hawkins becomes Treasurer of the Navy until his death.

SEARCH FOR THE WAY HOME

There is some argument surrounding the exact route home taken by Drake. Some claim that he did not touch land again after leaving Java until arriving back at Plymouth. Others believe he may have visited southern India before crossing the Indian Ocean. He is seen here supposedly paying homage to an Indian ruler.

THE *GOLDEN HIND*

Drake set sail from Plymouth on 13 December 1577 with five ships and a combined crew of 164. The flagship was the *Pelican*, a relatively small vessel of 120 tons and carrying just 18 cannon. The smallest ship, the *Benedict*, displaced just 15 tons, a tiny vessel to undertake so arduous a journey. About half-way into the journey, Drake abandoned two of his ships (probably because of high mortality amongst the crews). Of the other three, the *Marigold* perished and the *Elizabeth*, unbeknown to Drake, returned to England without completing the voyage. Only the flagship, renamed the *Golden Hind*, completed the circumnavigation.

KNIGHTHOOD

On Francis Drake's return from his circumnavigation of the world (1577-80) he was given a hero's welcome. He was knighted aboard his ship, the *Golden Hind*, by Elizabeth I the following year.

ILL FEELING

The serpent and beasts shown here are taken from a collection of engravings made to commemorate Drake's epic voyage. The serpent is a universal symbol of evil and bad luck, particularly amongst sailors. Drake's men would have encountered several on the trip, especially when making landfalls in South America, which would have made them very ill-at-ease. Drake kept his intended destination a secret from his men but when they eventually realised the truth discontent spread through the crews. They were incited to mutiny by Drake's one-time friend, Thomas Doughty, who was put on trial and executed.

...Drake's Circumnavigation of the World

Although usually credited as the second person to sail around the world (after Magellan, 1519-21), Drake actually deserves more credit for his feat than he is sometimes given. Magellan was the first European to cross the Pacific Ocean but he never completed the circumnavigation of

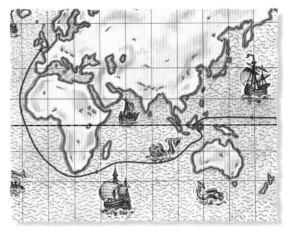

the world himself, though 18 members of his expedition did return to Spain aboard his ship the *Victoria*. It now seems likely that Magellan's original intention was simply to sail to the East Indies via the Pacific, and that it only became necessary to return home round the world to escape attack from the Portuguese. He was killed in the Philippines after completing about half of the journey, which means Drake was the first commander successfully to complete a circumnavigation himself.

EXOTIC NEW FOODS

It was impossible for Drake to take on board all the supplies he needed for his voyage, so rations were supplemented en route with exotic foods, such as the pineapple, which is a native fruit of Central and South America. Other foods from the tropics included coconuts, bananas and tomatoes. Drake brought these foods, among many others, back to England, where they quickly became eagerly sought as delicacies at table. Some could be grown in England, but pineapples could survive only in conservatories. Pineapples also became a favourite model for architectural features after this date.

SECRET VOYAGE

Shortly before embarking on his epic voyage, Drake was summoned to a secret meeting with Queen Elizabeth. She apparently instructed him to raid the unprotected Spanish ports on the west coast of South America. To that end Drake was extremely successful and brought his investors an incredible 4,700% profit. Elizabeth herself profited by £300,000. Drake's first words when he returned to Plymouth on 26 September 1580 were reputedly, 'Does the Queen still live?'

The New Colonies

The idea of establishing new colonies around the world came slowly to the Elizabethans. The original motivation for exploring new countries arose first out of trade and the need to establish new markets, and latterly from greed. Even the Spaniards, who actually invaded parts of Central and South America, had little thought of colonisation at first. What they craved was gold. England, Holland and France were quick to follow and readily plundered the Spanish ships returning home for their share of the booty. It was another 200 years before England made any serious attempts at building an empire. When it did come it followed the same pattern of establishing colonies around trading posts, with the result that the British Empire was scattered right across the globe along trade routes, rather than radiating out from a coherent centre.

VIRGINIA

England's first efforts at establishing colonies in North America failed, though they paved the way for later attempts and laid the foundations of what one day was to become the British Empire. Walter Raleigh established a small colony at Roanoke Island (now part of North Carolina) in 1584-5 and christened the territory 'Virginia', in honour of Elizabeth, the 'virgin queen'. Conditions proved too harsh and the colonists met with hostile reactions from the local Indians, resulting in the colony being deserted by 1590.

CONQUISTADORS

At the time of the first European colonisation of Central and South America, there were two dominant civilisations there: the Aztecs, centred in what is now Mexico, and the Incas of Peru and surrounding areas. Although technologically advanced, both societies were based on conquest and empire-building, rather than colonisation, and demanded tribute from those they defeated. Their society was one of domination, principally by high taxation to pay for monumental works, and their religions demanded sacrificial victims. When the Spanish conquered their lands in the 16th century, many of the ordinary people are said to have welcomed them, initially, as liberators rather than as conquerors (conquistadors).

FAILED COLONY

Following the failure of Raleigh's colony at Roanoke Island, no further attempts at colonisation were made by the Elizabethans. The colony of Virginia was eventually re-established further north and named Jamestown, after James I. This settlement was more successful, based on a thriving tobacco trade with England.

SAVED BY A PRINCESS

One of the early Virginian colonists, Captain John Smith, befriended an Indian princess, Pocahontas. Her father was Powhattan, said to be the king of all the Indian tribes in the area, who remained suspicious of the English. Powhattan decided to slay all the white colonists and return the land to Indian rule, but Pocahontas risked her life to warn Smith and so avoided a massacre.

POCAHONTAS

Although Pocahontas saved the life of John Smith, he was hurt in the struggle and was afterwards sent home to England. She later married another prominent colonist, John Rolfe, and returned to England with him, where she was received at King James I's court. Pocahontas persuaded Rolfe to let her return to America but, tragically, she died on the eve of her departure (2 May 1617) from either smallpox or a common cold at the age of 22 and is buried in Gravesend, Kent.

INDIANS' REVENGE

The Spanish conquerors of Central and South America overran the local Indians within the space of just two years. Unfortunately, before any real attempts at colonisation had been contemplated, the Spanish thirst for gold (which was in plentiful supply and was regarded by the Indians as only of decorative value) reached almost fever pitch. The conquerors openly pillaged the land, Mexico and Peru in particular, in their search for riches. Although initially welcomed by the Indians as saviours from a harsh military regime, the Spaniards soon took advantage and exploited the Indians, killing and torturing thousands. Then, they enslaved thousands more in the silver mines they discovered. Indians are here seen extracting their revenge by pouring molten gold down the throat of a captured conquistador.

THE SPANISH INVASION

One of the reasons for the speed with which Spain overran the Aztec and Inca empires is that many conquered Indian tribes, hostile to their old enemies, actively aided the Spanish soldiers. Another reason was the Spanish use of guns, which were unheard of in South America. Cortez conquered the Aztec civilisation in 1519-20, completely destroying their capital of Tenochtitlan in the process and building his own capital, Mexico City, on it's ruins.

New Trade Routes...

*T*he need to discover new trade routes during Elizabeth's reign grew directly out of England's on-going war with Spain. Spain was then the richest and most powerful country in Europe and had already extended her empire to much of the West Indies and Central America, jealously guarding the southern and western seaways. International trade was as important to the Elizabethan economy and society as it is to us today and so it became essential to open up new trade routes. Even though travelling by sea was hazardous, it was still preferable to overland transportation, which was hindered by poor roads and hostile countries. Drake and the other Elizabethan seafarers began by simply stealing Spanish treasure and other blatant acts of piracy, but soon the need to open up new and longer term trade routes became the priority.

SLAVE TRADE

The Spanish occupation of the Caribbean and South America had been ruthless and many natives were slain. Many of the survivors proved unsuitable or unwilling to be employed as labourers, so there was a ready market for slaves exported from West Africa.

The Spaniards strictly controlled the import of slaves into the colonies but English mariners, including Drake and Hawkins, engaged in illicit slave trading to the Spanish Main and afterwards to the new colonies of North America.

A SWEET TOOTH

Sugar had been available in England prior to the 16th century in the form of sugar-beet (a root vegetable) but extraction was laborious. Sugar cane yielded a much more productive crop but it would not grow in the English climate. Many sugar plantations were established in the West Indies, usually employing slave labour.

SOUTH CHINA SEAS

Opening up new trade routes was not without its problems. From the mid-16th century on, trade between the Far-East and Europe increased dramatically, so much so that heavily-laden merchant ships soon became prime targets for pirate attacks. The South China Seas between China, Japan and the East Indies were particularly treacherous. Sometimes fleets of pirate vessels descended upon merchant ships. Favourite vessels of Chinese pirates were captured trading junks, as shown here, converted to carry guns. Eventually, influential merchant companies (such as the East India Company) who financed the voyages, persuaded the British government to protect merchant shipping.

RUSSIA

In 1553 Sir Hugh Willoughby and Richard Chancellor set out to try to discover the North-East Passage. They became separated, Willoughby perished in the ice but Chancellor went on to reach the Russian coast and then travelled overland to Moscow (shown above) the following year. He set up trade relations (principally in furs) between Russia and England but died off Scotland on a return trip in 1555.

UNUSUAL FOODS

Many of the foods brought back by the Elizabethan seafarers were regarded as no more than interesting curiosities, such as the tomato, (bottom right). Others, like the potato, quickly became firm favourites at table to supplement the often limited diet at the time. They were usually quite expensive, however, and so were regarded more as a delicacy until botanists succeeded in introducing the plants to the English climate. The introduction of culinary spices brought back from abroad was welcomed. Peppers and chillies, from South America, (left) were used to disguise the often rancid taste of Elizabethan food, while from the East Indies came such flavourings as cloves. During Drake's circumnavigation he had to take on board many unusual and exotic foods to sustain his crews. Amongst these was the coconut palm, which natives used as a major source of food, making oil from the kernels. Drake brought a coconut back to England, which he presented to Elizabeth as a memento of his voyage. The tobacco plant (above right) came from North America, where the native Indians smoked it in clay pipes. Originally it was used as a medicine to purge the body of phlegm.

...New Trade Routes

SIR THOMAS GRESHAM
(c.1519-79)

The cost of voyages abroad was very high and could not have been undertaken without financial backing from rich merchants. One of the foremost was Sir Thomas Gresham, who built the Royal Exchange in London.

Elizabethan expeditions reached destinations as far apart as Russia, North America and Canada in the north, and South America, Africa and Asia in the south, looking for new trade routes. Their achievement was all the more incredible because of the length of time taken to complete the journeys in small vessels, often crossing uncharted seas. The importance of opening up new trade routes to Asia and the East Indies was paramount in the eyes of the Elizabethan merchant adventurers. Spices were the most prized and valuable commodity, fetching astronomical prices on the European markets.

The view shown here is of the tropical coast of Ceylon, now Sri Lanka, off the south-east coast of India.

THE BEGINNINGS OF AN EMPIRE

India and Ceylon had been known to European explorers since at least the time of Marco Polo (c.1295) and would have been familiar to the Elizabethan seafarers on their frequent visits to the Spice Islands. As elsewhere, the Elizabethans' prime concern was setting up new trade routes, but they frequently encountered strange new cultures, from primitive Indian witch doctors in North America (shown here) to the highly sophisticated and ancient cultures of Asia. In 1601 the East India Company received its royal charter, marking the beginning of Britain's first claims to an empire.

Life on Board

Life on board ship in Elizabethan times was extremely harsh and the pay (which was frequently in arrears) was very poor. But, faced with abject poverty on land at a time when many country people were being forcibly ejected from their land because of changing farming practices, many had little option. A fair proportion of a ship's crew would also have been criminals escaping justice, which often led to problems with discipline. The mortality rate amongst an average crew was very high and it would be considered normal for a ship to return to port with only a quarter of the men left alive. To ensure they had enough men left to make the return journey most captains oversubscribed when signing on a new crew, but this in itself led to problems of overcrowding and food rationing. Conditions on board were cramped, each man usually sleeping in a hammock slung below decks at his place of work, and toilet facilities were virtually non-existent.

JACK-OF-ALL-TRADES

A crew on an Elizabethan ship had to be completely self-sufficient, for they were often away at sea for several years and might go many months between landings. As well as being able to handle the ship sailors had to master other essential skills, such as carpentry, sailmaking, ropemaking and cooking.

DRUNKENNESS

One of the commonest problems facing any captain commanding an Elizabethan ship on a long voyage was boredom and the unruly behaviour of his crew. With fresh water in short supply the only drink available was beer (a gallon per crew member per day) or other stronger alcohols, which frequently led to drunkenness, not only on board but in port. Discipline was necessarily very harsh to avoid potentially fatal accidents at sea.

DISEASE

The most common form of disease encountered aboard ship was scurvy, a deficiency of vitamin C, caused by lack of fresh fruit and vegetables. The symptoms include bleeding into the skin and teeth loosening. Resistance to infection is also lowered, often resulting in death if untreated. All ships carried their share of rats, which might spread infectious diseases such as plague. Other common diseases were malaria, typhoid and dysentery.

THE CHATHAM CHEST

After the Armada of 1588, so many seamen were wounded and maimed that Sir John Hawkins established the 'Chatham Chest' - the first seaman's charity. All sailors in the Navy had to pay six pence a month from their wages into it for welfare purposes. This is the chest of 1625.

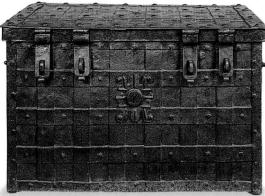

THE ART OF THE GUNNER

Most Elizabethan ships carried a number of cannon (a mortar is shown here), usually made from cast iron or bronze. They were mounted on carriages and secured in place by heavy ropes to control the recoil when being fired and to prevent them coming adrift in heavy seas. They were used mostly to disable a ship before boarding.

HEALTH & SAFETY

The health and safety of the crew aboard a typical Elizabethan ship was, to say the least, extremely hazardous. There were many accidents in simply carrying out the day-to-day tasks of sailing. Injuries sustained during encounters with enemy vessels, usually at close quarters, were horrific. Most ships carried a surgeon but the treatment he was able to administer was both limited and very crude. By far the most common form of treatment was the amputation of badly damaged or infected limbs. There was no anaesthetic (other than to make the patient drunk) and the survival rate was appallingly low. Many of those who survived surgery died from gangrene afterwards.

DAILY SUSTENANCE

All of the ship's food was prepared in the galley and then distributed among the crew. Food was rarely fresh and might consist of biscuit, salted beef or fish, supplemented by cheese and gruel, a kind of porridge mix. Drinking water was usually scarce but most ships carried a plentiful supply of beer. The pieces of tableware shown here were retrieved from Henry VIII's ship the *Mary Rose* and are typical of items in use throughout the Tudor period.

Navigation

In these days of radar, computer technology and satellites, it is easy to underestimate the great navigational skills of the Elizabethan seafarers. For the large part they were sailing uncharted seas and had to estimate their position as best they could, using only the positions of heavenly bodies to guide them. Until the development of more refined instruments, such as the chronometer in the mid-18th century, navigation was a very inexact science and relied heavily on the observational skills of the individual. Needless to say, there were many accidents, particularly if the ships were blown off-course by bad weather into unknown waters.

GUIDED BY THE STARS

During the 16th century the cross-staff became commonly used to calculate a ship's latitude (north-south position) at night. It comprised two pieces of wood, similar in appearance to a crossbow, with graduated scales marked along the length. By observing the angle between the horizon and the North (or Pole) Star and taking a reading off the scale, coupled with a compass reading, the ship's approximate position could be calculated. Shown here is a buckstaff, invented about 1594, for measuring the height of the sun for the same purpose.

THE 'MARINER'S MIRROUR'

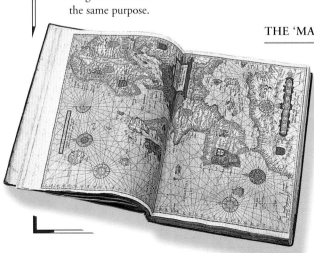

Following Magellan's, and later Drake's, circumnavigation of the world, it became possible more accurately to assess the Earth's size, which led in turn to the production of more accurate charts. The first sea atlas to be published in England, in 1588, was the *Mariner's Mirrour*. It was a collection of maps and charts showing the known coastlines of the world, derived from Dutch originals. The Dutch were at that time an English ally against Spain and at the forefront of navigational techniques.

LODESTONE

One of the main problems facing Elizabethan navigators was accurately calculating a ship's longitude (east-west position). Here, the astronomer-mathematician Flavius tries to do so by floating a piece of lodestone (a form of iron oxide) in a bowl of water, whilst making calculations.

STEERING BY THE SUN

This view shows an Elizabethan navigator trying to calculate the ship's latitude by use of a compass and an early form of quadrant to measure the angle of the sun's rays. However, precise time-keeping was necessary to ensure the accuracy of the calculations so at best a ship's position could only be approximated. The first fully successful sea-clock (chronometer) was not developed until 1759.

DRAKE'S DIAL

By Elizabethan times, compasses and other astronomical instruments had become quite sophisticated, as can be seen in this beautifully crafted astronomical compendium. It was made of brass in 1569 by Humphrey Cole, one of the finest scientific instrument makers of the time, and was once believed to have belonged to Drake himself. The compendium comprised a compass, along with lunar and solar dials which, as well as being an astronomical aid, enabled the user to calculate the time. Engraved on the casing were the latitudes of many important ports around the world.

SIR FRANCIS DRAKE
-A Time Line-

~1583~
Sir Humphrey Gilbert claims Newfoundland for England.

~1584~
Walter Raleigh establishes the first colony in Virginia.

~1585~
Drake sacks Santiago.

Drake sets sail for West Indies, his first command as Admiral.

~1587~
Mary Queen of Scots executed.

GETTING YOUR BEARINGS

The ancient Chinese discovered that lodestone is naturally magnetic and if suspended on a string will always point to the north. Early navigators made good use of this natural material but it was somewhat crude. Sometime in the 12th century, European navigators discovered that a needle could be similarly magnetised by stroking it with a lodestone. This discovery eventually led to the development of more sophisticated and accurate compasses, with the needle balanced on a central pivot. The example shown here is encased in an ivory bowl and dates from about 1580.

PITCHED BATTLE

Commander of the English fleet sent to stop
the Armada was Lord Howard of Effingham.
A week-long pitched battle took place in
the Channel but the English could
not halt the progress of the Spanish.
The battle turned in favour of the
English, however, when Drake
launched eight fire-ships into the
Armada off Gravelines (north of
Calais), which threw the Spanish
into disarray. The following
day the Armada was routed
and fled into the
North Sea.

The Spanish Armada

ollowing Henry VIII's break with the Church of Rome in 1533, England was under constant threat from the Catholic countries of Europe to re-establish papal authority. Spain was particularly enraged at the acts of open piracy on her ships by English adventurers, especially during Elizabeth I's reign, and so needed little persuading to launch an offensive against England. In July 1588 a massive armada of 138 ships and 24,000 men was sent to invade England.

ARMADA MEDAL

This gold medal, commemorating England's victory over the Armada, was awarded to each of the commanders of the English fleet.

THE ARMADA APPROACHES

According to an unsubstantiated legend, Drake is supposed to have insisted on finishing his game of bowls before putting out to sea. The Spanish Armada created a formidable spectacle as it advanced slowly up the Channel. The English fleet was hampered by the tide in rapidly getting its ships into open waters but the daring seamanship of Drake, Vice-Admiral John Hawkins, Martin Frobisher and many others eventually won the day.

Drake ~ Later Life

DRAKE'S LAST VOYAGE

Drake's last, ill-fated voyage took place in 1595-6. He and John Hawkins were commanded to attack Puerto Rico, to cut off Spain's supply of treasure ships. There was friction between the two admirals from the start, which came to a head when Drake decided to make an excursion to the Canary Islands (above) for supplies. The attack failed, but worse was to come. A messenger ship was sent from the Canaries to warn the governor of Puerto Rico of the intended attack. The island's defences had been sadly lacking and would probably have succumbed to Drake and Hawkins. But with two weeks' warning the Spaniards were able to make the necessary preparations and in the event the English attack failed dismally. Hawkins died before the attack was launched and Drake about a month later, of dysentery, on 25 January 1596, off Porto Bello.

Although Drake has often been accused of being a ne'er-do-well who was little better that a legalised pirate, acting as Elizabeth's agent in her war with Spain, such criticism is perhaps a little harsh. He was, by all accounts, an honourable man, who took good care of his crews, even if sometimes using rough methods. He certainly hankered after the finer things in life and, following his knighthood in 1581, regarded himself as a member of the new aristocracy. This earned him many enemies among those with inherited titles. After his circumnavigation, he became Mayor of Plymouth and campaigned for many improvements to the town, including a better water supply. A short man of stocky build, he is said to have become quite portly in later life, and settled into semi-retirement at Buckland Abbey, near his birthplace. This had been seized by the crown at the dissolution and converted into a fine house by Sir Richard Grenville.

DRAKE'S DRUM

'Take my drum to England, hang et by the shore,
Strike et when your powder's runnin' low;
If the Dons sight Devon, I'll quit the port o' Heaven,
An' drum them up the Channel as we drummed them long ago'

These lines are an extract from a poem by Sir Henry Newbolt. The drum was used aboard the *Golden Hind* to muster the crew for battle. On his deathbed Drake, according to legend, promised to return and fight for England if ever the drum were beaten at the approach of an enemy.

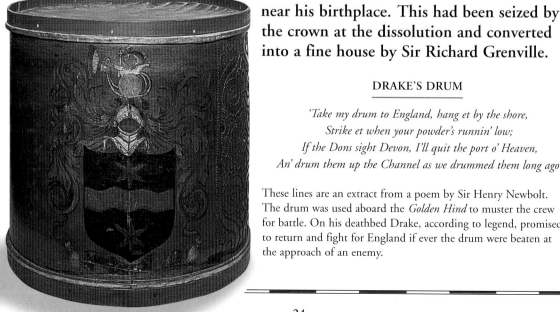

BRILLIANT STRATEGIST

Throughout his illustrious career Drake had struck fear into the hearts of the Spaniards. In 1587 he executed a flawless attack on Cadiz harbour, where he was said to have 'singed the King of Spain's beard' by destroying 37 (the Spanish claimed it was 24) galleons gathering to form an armada to be sent against England. The following year, of course, he was instrumental in defeating the 'Great Armada' itself and in between times he was a constant threat to Spanish shipping in the Caribbean. An expert navigator, he revolutionised naval strategy by taking the fight to the enemy. When Philip II of Spain heard news of his death he is said to have openly rejoiced.

FALL FROM FAVOUR

In 1583 Drake's first wife died and soon after he married Elizabeth Sydenham, who outlived him, but he had no children by either wife. He engaged in a few expeditions following his circumnavigation but he gradually slipped into semi-retirement following the defeat of the Armada in 1588 and spent more and more time either in London, at court, or in his new official duties at Plymouth. During that time he rather fell from favour, and Martin Frobisher superseded him as Elizabeth's shining star.

The Elizabethan Explorers...

*T*he 'age of discovery' by European explorers really began in Portugal, in 1415, with Prince Henry, known as Henry the Navigator. He sent ships out to explore the north and west coasts of Africa, bringing back such riches as ivory. Vasco da Gama (c.1460-1524), also Portuguese, rounded the Cape of Good Hope, off the southernmost tip of Africa, and went on to open the first European maritime route to India. Later Portuguese explorers went on to discover routes to Japan, south-east Asia and South America, which soon made Portugal one of the wealthiest nations in Europe. Spain, and later England, emulated these first voyages in their thirst for gold and other riches, most of which (except in the Far East) were plundered from the native inhabitants of the countries they visited. Apart from advances made in compiling more accurate navigational charts, very little scientific data was gathered on these early voyages, which were primarily motivated by money and trade.

ARAB INFLUENCE

Arab explorers from north Africa greatly extended their empire from the 6th to the 13th centuries, as far as northern Spain. They sailed the Mediterranean and the Indian Ocean in small boats called dhows. They developed sophisticated astronomical equipment, such as this astrolabe, which greatly influenced European mariners.

JOHN CABOT (c.1450-c.99)

The quest for new trade routes in Tudor England really began with Henry VII. He considered sponsoring Christopher Columbus on his voyage of discovery to the New World, but chose instead to finance an expedition by the Italian John Cabot, who tried to find a new route to China and the Spice Islands via the fabled North-West Passage. He believed he had reached China when he struck land, but it was in fact the coast of Newfoundland. He is seen here departing from Bristol in 1497.

CHURCH MISSIONARIES

Although the prime objective of the early explorers had been money, with no real interest in colonisation, the church had different views. Within a few years of the first expeditions, Christian missionaries were established to convert the pagan natives. Many fell victim to the Indians, like the Franciscan missionaries shown here being eaten by North American cannibals.

THE SHIPWRIGHT'S SKILL

One of the reasons given for England's superiority at sea over Spain is the design of her warships. Sir John Hawkins was responsible for introducing revolutionary new designs by Matthew Baker and Peter Pett, which completely transformed the English navy. The new ships were smaller and sleeker than the cumbersome Spanish galleons. They were low at the bows, but high at the stern, which made them much more manoeuvrable.

CELESTIAL GLOBE

This Flemish celestial globe of c.1537 shows the somewhat limited understanding of the constellations in the skies of the southern hemisphere in Tudor times. Information gathered from the round-the-world voyages of Magellan, Drake and Cavendish was added later, but this lack of knowledge made any journey in the southern oceans particularly hazardous.

SIR FRANCIS DRAKE
-A TIME LINE-

~1587~
The Spanish decide to launch offensive against England.

Drake sacks the port of Cadiz - 'singeing the King of Spain's beard'.

~1588~
Spanish Armada sent against England, and defeated in the Channel after week-long running battle.

~1591~
Sir Richard Grenville of the Revenge *dies after being outnumbered by a Spanish fleet in the Azores.*

NO SMOKE WITHOUT FIRE

While Raleigh is popularly credited with introducing potatoes and tobacco to England from the New World, that honour is now usually given to his contemporary, Sir John Hawkins. He did make smoking fashionable at court, however, where he was one of Elizabeth I's favourites. Tobacco was usually smoked in long clay pipes, similar to the pipes used by American Indians. Raleigh is seen here being doused with water by one of his servants, who feared he was on fire!

SIR WALTER RALEIGH
(c.1552-1618)

Sir Walter Raleigh was a soldier, courtier and explorer. He was a keen exponent of establishing English colonies in the New World, including Virginia, but they all failed. When James I acceded to the throne he was accused of treason and imprisoned.

SIR JOHN HAWKINS (1532-95)

Sir John Hawkins, a distant relative of Drake, was responsible for modernising Elizabeth's navy and played a major role in defeating the Spanish Armada. After the Armada many of the crews were unpaid and, together with Drake, he set up a fund for distressed seamen called the Chatham Chest. He is said to have introduced the potato and tobacco into England. He died in 1595 during his and Drake's last, ill-fated Caribbean voyage.

SIR FRANCIS DRAKE
-A Time Line-

~1593~
Battle of Ballishannon in Ireland.

~1594~
Martin Frobisher dies.

~1595~
Drake sets off to attack Puerto Rico (his last voyage) with John Hawkins.

Sir John Hawkins dies.

~1596~
Drake dies of dysentery at Porto Bello in the Caribbean.

THE SEARCH FOR EL DORADO

In 1616, whilst still in prison, Raleigh persuaded James I to let him lead an expedition (his second) to the Orinoco River in Guiana, to search for the fabled El Dorado (city of gold). The voyage failed and Raleigh came home in disgrace. He was executed in 1618 under the original terms of his sentence.

...The Elizabethan Explorers...

The world in the 15th century was much more fragmented than we would recognise today. Areas of advanced civilisation existed in many places, including North Africa, the Mediterranean, China and India, but each had only a limited knowledge of the existence of the others. Few Europeans at that time had any awareness of the world beyond Europe itself. Legends and travellers' tales abounded, so that even those who did venture further afield were seldom believed. The Atlantic was largely unexplored and the existence of America and the Pacific Ocean beyond had not been proved. Much of the world remained a mystery, uncharted and unmapped. For the brave adventurers setting out on their voyages of discovery, with only limited navigational skills, it was a journey into the unknown, akin to our own space explorations to the moon and beyond.

SIR RICHARD GRENVILLE (c 1541-91)

Sir Richard Grenville was another who advocated the colonisation of the New World rather than simply making piratical raids on Spanish treasure ships. He is best remembered for his gallant fight off Flores, in the Azores, in 1591. He was commander of the *Revenge*, Drake's former flagship against the Armada, and when he found himself surrounded by Spanish vessels, he insisted on carrying on the fight alone. A harsh, arrogant man, he was fatally wounded and ordered the ship to be scuttled rather than give it up to the Spanish, but his crew insisted on surrendering instead. Grenville died aboard the Spanish flagship shortly afterwards.

SIR HUMPHREY GILBERT (c 1539-83)

Sir Humphrey Gilbert was another leading exponent of establishing English colonies in the New World. In 1578 he received Letters Patent from the queen authorising him to colonise new lands. Finally, in 1583, he gathered sufficient support and set off for Newfoundland. At St. John's, already a flourishing port, he formally claimed the territory for England. He died on the way home, leaving his half-brother, Walter Raleigh, to finish his task.

...The Elizabethan Explorers

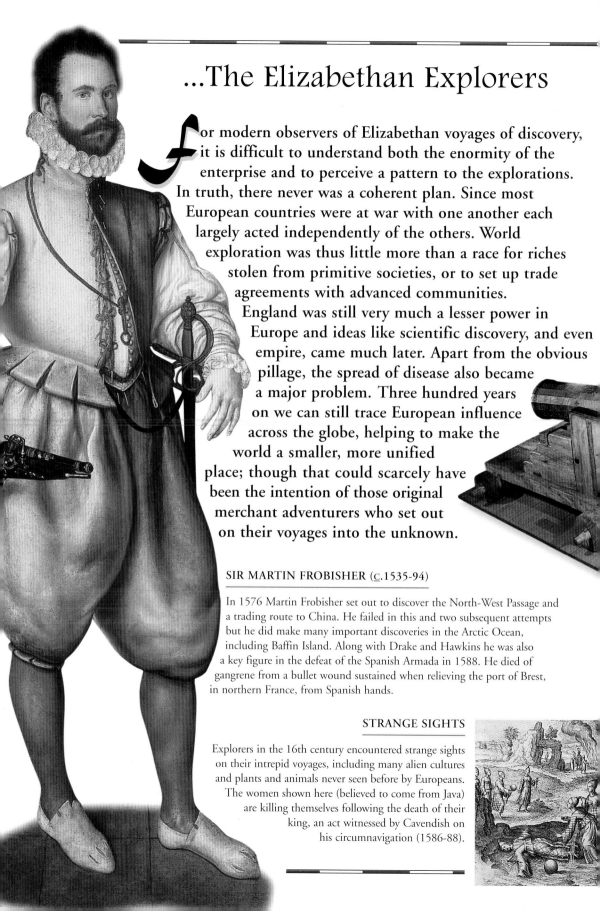

for modern observers of Elizabethan voyages of discovery, it is difficult to understand both the enormity of the enterprise and to perceive a pattern to the explorations. In truth, there never was a coherent plan. Since most European countries were at war with one another each largely acted independently of the others. World exploration was thus little more than a race for riches stolen from primitive societies, or to set up trade agreements with advanced communities.

England was still very much a lesser power in Europe and ideas like scientific discovery, and even empire, came much later. Apart from the obvious pillage, the spread of disease also became a major problem. Three hundred years on we can still trace European influence across the globe, helping to make the world a smaller, more unified place; though that could scarcely have been the intention of those original merchant adventurers who set out on their voyages into the unknown.

SIR MARTIN FROBISHER (c.1535-94)

In 1576 Martin Frobisher set out to discover the North-West Passage and a trading route to China. He failed in this and two subsequent attempts but he did make many important discoveries in the Arctic Ocean, including Baffin Island. Along with Drake and Hawkins he was also a key figure in the defeat of the Spanish Armada in 1588. He died of gangrene from a bullet wound sustained when relieving the port of Brest, in northern France, from Spanish hands.

STRANGE SIGHTS

Explorers in the 16th century encountered strange sights on their intrepid voyages, including many alien cultures and plants and animals never seen before by Europeans. The women shown here (believed to come from Java) are killing themselves following the death of their king, an act witnessed by Cavendish on his circumnavigation (1586-88).

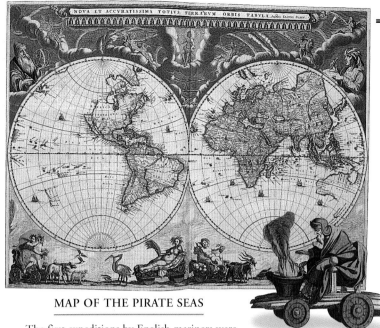

MAP OF THE PIRATE SEAS

The first expeditions by English mariners were little more than acts of legalised piracy. Elizabeth I instructed her sea captains to intercept as many Spanish treasure ships as possible and steal their gold. Afterwards, when the expeditions became more legitimate, the seas remained infested by pirates, opportunist cut-throats who attacked any ship and plundered its cargo.

ARMAMENTS

Most ships in the 16th century carried a small number of guns, similar to this bronze demi-cannon retrieved from the wreck of the *Mary Rose*, which sank in 1545. It was one of the first English warships to be equipped with gunports cut into her sides. Cannon of this type were usually cast from iron or bronze and remained the principal form of armament on fighting ships for the next 300 years.

THOMAS CAVENDISH (1560-92)

Shortly after Drake's return from his circumnavigation of the world, Thomas Cavendish was commissioned to emulate his epic voyage. He completed the journey in less time than Drake (1586-88) but largely followed the same route. His was probably the first intentional voyage of circumnavigation. Both Magellan's and Drake's voyages appear to have had other motives, at least initially, and both were forced to complete their circumnavigation as the safest route home. In 1591 Cavendish set out again for the East Indies but the voyage ended in disaster. Through the Straits of Magellan the men killed penguins for sustenance, which putrefied, over-running the ship with worms. Soon afterwards a particularly nasty bout of scurvy broke out, killing about 75% of the crew.

SIR FRANCIS DRAKE
-A Time Line-

~1598~
Philip II, King of Spain, dies.

~1600~
Will Adams becomes the first Englishman to land in Japan.

~1603~
Elizabeth I (last Tudor monarch) dies and is succeeded by James I.

~1603~
Raleigh arrested for treason.

~1609~
Hudson's first expedition to North America.

~1616~
Raleigh sets out to discover El Dorado but fails and returns to England in disgrace.

~1618~
Sir Walter Raleigh executed for treason.

DID YOU KNOW?

How the Spice Islands got their name?
One of the main attractions for the Elizabethan explorers searching for new trade routes were spices from the East. The groups of islands that make up the East Indies (which include the Moluccas, Philippines and Melanesia groups of islands) were particularly rich in such commodities and came to be known collectively as the Spice Islands.

That of all the continents Antarctica is the coldest, driest, highest and windiest? It covers an area half as large again as the U.S.A. (about 5.5 million square miles) and represents one-tenth of the Earth's land mass. Approximately 98% of Antarctica is covered by ice, up to a mile and a half thick in places. The Elizabethan explorers had searched in vain for a habitable land mass in the southern oceans, which was not finally discovered until 1820 when Edward Bransfield landed on part of the Antarctic Peninsula.

Where the term 'a square meal' comes from? It is not known when this term first came into use but since at least Tudor times meals on board ship were dished up on square platters, which seamen balanced on their laps. They had frames around the edge to prevent the food from falling off and were so shaped to enable them to be easily stored when not in use. Each sailor thus received his full ration, or square meal, for the day.

How America got its name? America was named after the 16th-century navigator and mapmaker Amerigo Vespucci. Of Italian birth, in 1508 he was created Chief Royal Pilot of Spain.

All Spanish captains had to provide him with full details each time they undertook a new voyage so that he could constantly amend and update his collection of sea charts. He made several voyages to the New World himself (notably in 1499-1500) and was once credited with discovering America. Although this was not true, he was the first to consider it to be an independent continent and not part of Asia. It was afterwards known as 'Amerigo's Land' in honour of him.

That legends associated with Drake's Drum (*see page 24*) are still being created?
During World War II stories circulated of warships supposedly carrying Drake's Drum that were miraculously saved from disaster after the ghostly sounds of drumming were heard. In truth, the drum has never been carried aboard any ship since its return to England in the 16th century and during the Second World War it was locked away for safe-keeping. Replicas may have been carried aboard ships, but not the original, which shows just how easily stories can generate, especially if spread by word of mouth.

That we still use the stars to navigate by?
It is easy to assume that because navigational techniques used in the past were relatively simple they were also inaccurate. This is not necessarily true, although results need to be accurately recorded and verified to be usable. In 1967 astronomers discovered pulsars, rapidly rotating condensed stars (formed from dead stars) that emit radio waves, or pulses, as detectable beams. They pulsate at fixed rates making it possible for future space programmes to utilise them for navigational purposes in outer space.

ACKNOWLEDGEMENTS

Consultant Editor: Pieter van der Merwe, National Maritime Museum. We would also like to thank: Graham Rich, Peter Done and Elizabeth Wiggins for their assistance and David Hobbs for his map of the world.
Picture research by Image Select. Printed in Hong Kong. Copyright © 1998 ticktock Publishing Ltd.
First published in Great Britain by ticktock Publishing Ltd., The Offices in the Square, Hadlow, Tonbridge, Kent, TN11 0DD, U.K., in association with the National Maritime Museum, Greenwich. All rights reserved.
No part of this publication may be reproduced, stored in a retrieval system, or transmitted in any form or by any means, electronic, mechanical, photocopying, recording or otherwise, without prior written permission of the copyright owner.
A CIP Catalogue for this book is available from the British Library. ISBN 1 86007 031 0

Picture Credits: t=top, b=bottom, c=centre, l=left, r=right
Aisa (Barcelona): IFC 1 tl, 12 tl. Ann Ronan / Image Select (London): 18/19 cb. Bridgeman (London): 3 tl, 3 bl, 25 cr, 28 cb. The Golden Hinde Ltd (London): 10/11 c & OFC. Image Select: 8 bl, 15 tr. Mary Evans Picture Library: 1 tr, 3 cr, 4 t, 5 br, 6 c, 6 tr, 6/7 c, 6/7 cb, 7 br, 8/9 cb, 9 cb, 10 t, 10 bl, 12 bl & 13 br, 13 t, 12/13 cb, 14 tl & OFC, 14 bl, 15 r & OFC, 16/17, 16 t & OBC, 17 tl & OFC, 18 tl, 18 bl, 19 c, 21 tr, 20/21 ct, 22 tr & OBC, 24 tl, 24/25 c, 25 tr, 26 bl, 28 tr & OBC, 28/29 cb, 30/31 cb, 31 br, 32 c. National Maritime Museum (London): IFC, 25 l & tr & 32 c, 2 br, 3 bl, 5 cl, 8 cl, 10 br, 11 br & OFC, 12/13 c & OFC, 14/15 c & OBC, 18/19 ct & OBC, 19 tr, 20 tl, 20/21 c & OBC, 21 br & OBC, 20 tl, 20 bl, 22/23, 23 tr, 22 cr, 24 bl & OBC, 26 tl, 26/27 cb, OFC & IFC, 27 t, 28 tl, 28 c & OBC, 29 br, 30 l, 30/31 c, 31t. PIX: 4 br, 9 c. Spectrum Colour Library: 13 tr. Courtesy of The Ulster Museum (Belfast): 8/9 c. West Devon Borough Council: 2 bl.

Every effort has been made to trace the copyright holders and we apologise in advance for any unintentional omissions.
We would be pleased to insert the appropriate acknowledgement in any subsequent edition of this publication.

snapping-turtle
guide